Finding Your Voice

Finding Your Voice

A collection of inspirational stories,
poems, thoughts, and quotes
to help you find your true voice

ORIGINAL WORKS BY
G. BRIAN BENSON

B dog Publishing
Las Vegas, Nevada

B dog Publishing
Las Vegas, Nevada
www.gbrianbenson.com

ISBN: 978-0-9822286-9-2

FRONT COVER PHOTO BY
MICHAEL SPROEHNLE-BENSON
INSIDE PHOTOS BY G. BRIAN BENSON AND
MICHAEL SPROEHNLE-BENSON

Brian's keen ability to listen to his heart and to follow his intuition has laid the blueprint for all of his successful projects and has served as an example for others to follow. In the modern world where the challenges seem to keep building up and the answers to those challenges often seem farther and farther away, his guidelines for helping everyone develop their own ability to listen and follow their inner wisdom is truly a potent and powerful way to find the guidance we all need.

—Mark Allen, six-time Hawaiian Ironman World Champion and author of *Fit Soul, Fit Body: 9 Keys to a Healthier, Happier You*

Being happy and healthy is not about fitting into the little black dress or owning the latest gadgets. Rather, it is about finding our true, authentic beings. Through his own personal journey, Brian has come to understand this truth and willingly shares what he has learned along the path of his own journey.

—Donna Morin, M.Ed, CHHC, wellness coach, writer, speaker, founder of Better Off Well

Brian's ability to write from the core of his being sets him apart from other writers. His real life experience and unique insights into what makes people tick and how to motivate and inspire them to better their lives is unique and powerful.

—Dina Proctor, author of *Madly Chasing Peace: How I Went from Hell to Happy in Nine Minutes a Day*

Brian's wisdom and positive attitude have been a constant source of encouragement to me for several years. I am so fortunate to have met him in person and realize that what he writes is 100% genuine. Brian lives and writes from his heart. There is no fluff or pretense. His writing is genuine inspiration from a truly inspiring person.
—Katrina Mayer, motivational speaker and author of *The Mustard Seed Way* and *Wholarian Vision*

In this complex world, straightforward talk that will improve your life step by easily done step, is rare. Brian takes us on yet another ever so worthwhile journey to our own fulfillment. His work exemplifies the old adage that "Just because it's worthwhile, doesn't mean it has to be hard to do." Brian makes it clear in his work that our steps to success can be both fun and easy while at the same time effective. Thanks, Brian!
—Tom Wright, A Course In Shamanism and the author of *One, The Answer, How Anger Makes Me Happy* and *Be Bad! Do Good!*

Few of us are brave enough to trust and follow our hearts. I am truly grateful to Brian for being such an inspiration and providing solutions in the most pure and simplistic form. He has been an inspirational guest on my talk show on several occasions and has continued to invite the audience to live life to its fullest potential. I know he will raise the vibration of the reader and provide them with tools and techniques to free themselves from whatever is holding them back.
—Elizabeth Cuckson, producer and host of Healing Hearts Radio, author, and inspirational speaker

To my brother Jeff.
Your courage I find very inspiring.
Thank you for being you.

‚Ç

We are all here to learn about ourselves and
inspire others in our own unique way.

G. Brian Benson

Welcome and thank you for purchasing this collection of inspirational stories, thoughts, poems and quotes that I have compiled for you. These all came from my heart and played an important role in my own personal growth experience. I hope that they resonate with you as much as they have with me. We are here to learn, grow and help each other as we move through life. Please continue to let your inner greatness out and allow it to shine for all to see! It will be the best thing you ever did.

Sincerely, Brian

Contents

Light

Can you see your light inside you?
It shines both day and night
Leading you both near and far
Keeping your path in sight

Can you feel your light inside you?
As it courses through your veins
Inspired greatness housed within
To share for all to gain

Can you taste your light inside you?
Flavored sweet and pure
Water, land and truthful food
Grant energy and cures

Can you hear your light inside you?
As it speaks to you in song
Guiding you to flow each day
Helping you stay strong

Can you touch your light inside you?
Compassion, joy and heat
A tender kiss, a warm embrace
Rituals to be complete

Can you sense your light inside you?
It's spoken from within

Hunches, feelings, heart-felt signs
Giving life a whole new spin

Will you trust your light inside you?
Your gifts, your being, your core
True greatness lay in wait
To be shared, enjoyed, explored

G. BRIAN BENSON 2011

Being out in nature reminds me that
everything is going to be okay.

G. BRIAN BENSON

Participation = Growth

When we are younger, we have a tendency to disregard others who are just participating. We sometimes think that glory should only be given to those who are the fastest or most accomplished. That is the furthest thing from the truth. We all are participants. Everyone has a different story or situation that they are playing out; whether it is in a triathlon race, a job or the classroom of life. I belonged in that triathlon not because I got out of the swim portion before some of the other participants or because I had a faster time on the bike than four other guys in my age group. I belonged because I was trying to learn about myself.

Life is all about trying to learn about oneself. I just chose the sport of triathlon and a race held in Cottage Grove, Oregon in 1987 to do my exploring. It took me awhile to learn this, but when I did, it opened my world up to wanting to help others learn about themselves and be the best that they can be as well. There is something very special about breaking personal barriers. If we hold it in gratitude and with the right attitude, others bear witness that they too can grow and live out their dreams. When we hold it to ourselves and don't understand that we are all part of the greater good, then it feels very shallow and empty.

There will always be someone who does something better than you. Don't run yourself into the ground trying to be better than that person. Set your goals and dreams for yourself and the growth that will come with your journey. All we can do is be better than we used to be. That is where true happiness comes from.

G. Brian Benson 2012

We Are Meant to Succeed

Have you ever felt whiney, angry or sad?
Or tired and frustrated and then acted bad?
You're not alone; we've all been there before
When we're all out of sorts and acted quite poor

Take heart and take heed, it's the balance of life
Some days were quite happy, others feeling some strife
The key to this game, is to understand how it's played
When you know what to expect, your confusion will fade

Love flows in balance; it's where we should be
Not too high, not to low, but the middle you see
Be thankful and happy for where you are at
Life here's for learning; it's as simple as that

So during those times when it's tough or unsure
Take a step back and think thoughts good or pure
Remember a time when you had some success
Believe in yourself and never ever second guess

Your life is perfection, the good times and bad
The easy and the tough, the happy and the sad
Each challenge brings a chance, to grow and become whole
To learn from your mistakes, and reconnect with your soul

We are meant to succeed, so take heart and take flight
Throw out your fears and give way to love's light
Your destiny beckons, your true nature at hand
Live life to its fullest, it's fantastic and grand!

G. Brian Benson 2008

To truly open your heart is to
truly remember who you are.

G. Brian Benson

What Is Your Dream?

Do you have a dream that you want to accomplish? Of course you do. So have I. We all have goals and dreams. What is your dream and what is holding you back from attaining it? Is your dream at the forefront of your existence or has it been tucked away and forgotten? Well, for starters let's get it back into your mindset and honor that it is something that is important to you and that you believe in. It isn't going to manifest itself. It needs fuel! Your dream is calling out to you and saying make me a part of your life. Think about me! Believe in me! Bring me to fruition!

How can we feed your dream? What is the fuel that will make it go? First of all you need to believe in your dream. You need to make it feel important and that it has to be a part of your life. I mean you need to taste it! I want you to imagine what your life will feel like when your dream becomes a reality. Will it make you feel happy? Satisfied? Fulfilled? Of course it will! You know what else it will do? It will give you the confidence to make another goal or dream become a reality. Why is this? Because you will have the momentum flowing from your initial realized goal or dream. I think you can see where this is going . . . each successful accomplishment will breed a stronger confidence within yourself which will lead to more success! Before you know it, you will be living a life of true fulfillment and actualized dreams. What more could you ask for?

What is your dream? I know that you have one. Every single one of us has a dream or dreams. I want you to realize your dream! I want you to test yourself, believe in yourself, listen to your intuition and live your dreams just like I have! We are wired to live a magical life! It is our true nature to follow our dreams and meet them with success. I will ask you again . . . what is your dream and what is holding you back?

G. Brian Benson 2009

My Dream

I have a dream, that your dream came true
That your world has changed, and you're enjoying the view
Your sun shines brighter, your confidence grows
There's a bounce in your step, your life is in flow

I have a dream, that your dream came true
Your ideas and vision are shiny and new
Your belief in yourself comes straight from the heart
Never again will it be, separate or apart

I have a dream, that your dream came true
By following your heart, you've been given your due
Your intuition is cherished, trusted and right
Your future lay sunny, inspired and bright

I have a dream, that your dream came true
That you're in control and have all the clues
You're an inspiration to others, as you play your true part
You live from your center, and you lead with your heart

G. Brian Benson 2009

It takes a lot to get through life sometimes . . .
but that doesn't mean it won't get better.

G. BRIAN BENSON

Are You Afraid of Success?

Who could possibly be afraid of success? Believe it or not, more people than you think. We are trained from a very early age by our parents, families, peers and society that there is a comfort in familiarity. You know ... go to school, find a job, get married, have kids, raise them and then retire. And what this training does to us is create habits in our lives that can sometimes be very hard to break. Especially if we have very close ties to our parents, families and peers. Now I am not saying that the route I just described is not right for you. We are all here to learn and there are many different paths to acquire said learning. And there can be much love and joy following this particular route. But what I am saying is that many of us are held back from moving forward and living out our dreams and goals because of the way we were taught and the habits that we have formed that were passed down to us. The way that old habits get in the way of achieving success is pretty simple. Many of us have been taught by our loved ones (and they were as well) that happiness and fulfillment comes from fitting into the societal mode that I described earlier. And unfortunately that sometimes clashes with the information that we are receiving from our heart and intuition. So, many of us are caught in a situation of feeling like we are letting our loved ones down by following our heart. Make sense? It's a big game of tug of war between our hearts and following our dreams against the guilt and fear of letting our loved ones down.

Unfortunately many people are afraid of breaking that habit or learned way of thinking and never step out and live their dreams. It's quite sad actually. If this sounds like a situation you are struggling with please know that you can still follow your heart and receive the love and acceptance from your families, peers and friends. I know this from personal experience. For 11 years (from 1997–2008) I managed a family business. I give thanks for the experience because it has made me who I am today, but it wasn't what I truly wanted to do. I always felt that I wouldn't be doing it forever and knew one day that I needed to leave and do something on my own. That day came in 2008 when my father and I sold our business. I was lucky that he understood my need to be on my own and follow my heart into writing and speaking. Not sure if he thought it a smart decision, but at least he understood. For most of the time that I was there running the business I felt some guilt and fear about the feelings I was having about wanting to do something else. In my mind I tried to make sense of it by saying, "wow, I was given this great opportunity to co-own and run my own business. What a loving gesture by my father." And it was a loving gesture. But my heart was telling me other things. It was telling me this wasn't fulfilling to me and that I needed to follow my true path. So you can see where sometimes it can be a bit tricky to follow ones heart. I have so much love for my family and it got in the way a little bit of me being my true authentic self. But in the end it always must be that way.

It is basically fear that is holding everyone in that position of believing it has to be a certain way. Break that myth! By showing them strength and honoring your gifts and intentions it will help them break the chain of fear and misunderstood ways of thinking. You don't have to be afraid of success. Like I said before it is your birthright! Be a trailblazer and show your friends and family that is it ok to step outside the old ways of thinking and be successful and shine!

G. BRIAN BENSON 2009

The full measure of our personal happiness is dictated by how much we offer of ourselves in helping others.

G. BRIAN BENSON

Time to Move On . . .

Ever have that feeling that it was time to move on from something? Could have been a job, a relationship or even a way of life that you had been living that didn't work for you anymore? I remember feeling very strongly four years ago that it was time for me to leave the family business. It had provided me a nice living and some security, but I just felt like I wasn't growing there anymore and that scared me. My life had lost its spark. I knew I had to leave.

Although I was a bit apprehensive at first having this familiar door close and leaving behind all that I knew . . . the beauty of life meant that another door was soon about to open. So I put my trust into the intuitive hunches that I was receiving and stepped into the unknown. And you know what? It was the best thing that I ever did for myself. After selling the business, I found myself living in a new city near my son who was about to enter high school. Really getting to know him the last four years has been the highlight of my life. In addition to bonding with my son, I was able to find a new voice with writing and honoring the gifts that I have been given. What more could I ask for?

When we take a leap of faith and honor our truths and hunches, magic truly can occur. Yes, stepping into the unknown can be a bit scary . . . but it can also be very liberating. We just need to trust in our feelings as we step into the unknown. I am reminded of a beautiful quote by Anais Nin where she said, "there came a time when the risk to remain tight in the bud was more painful than the risk it took to blossom." Only you can determine which one of these two pains is greater. I do know that the pain that comes with breaking out and blossoming is quite sweeter and has much more hope associated with it. For me . . . the pain in staying with the family business was much greater and I had to release it by leaving.

So I find myself once again wanting to open a new door. I want to continue to make myself available to grow, expand my horizons and share my gifts. Currently being single and having my son now make the transition to being an adult . . . I find myself with new options and a sense of freedom. You know we all are meant to share our gifts. And that can happen in so many different ways. But we need to put ourselves out there to make those connections to share. And to put ourselves "out there" certainly doesn't mean you have to move or quit your job either. It simply means to make a commitment to yourself to grow, honor who you are and be open to cultivating and sharing your gifts.

So where will I end up? I honestly don't know the answer to that question quite yet. I do know that Reno has felt like my home for the last 4 years and I will be always grateful for the friendships that I have made the natural beauty of the area and for the personal growth that I have gone through. I felt much supported here and know that many of the friendships that I cultivated in Reno will be for life. I also know that I am open to anything and everything going forward. It's a great way to be . . . one never knows what just might be right around that next corner.

So as I move forward into this new chapter of my life, I will tap into the excitement of the unknown and also give thanks for what I have learned and where I have been. This allows me to flow effortlessly going forward with no regrets and only positives in my back pocket. You can certainly do the same thing as you move forward in your life.

G. BRIAN BENSON 2012

Treasure Map

In search of treasure, we look for a map
A guide to riches fulfilled
An outline to lead us, a smooth road to travel
A sketch for happiness to yield

We search high to the heavens and low to the earth
For reasons to quiet our mind
We look near to friends and far to religion
For explanations and answers to find

Our path can be difficult and filled with much pain
As we seek away from our heart
A route void of aim, light or guidance
And back to the beginning we start

So we gather our strength and give try again
And begin to roll with the tide
The treasure we seek isn't high, low, near or far
But in us, resting gently inside

G. Brian Benson 2011

Peace and strength through balance.

G. BRIAN BENSON

Back in the Saddle Again

Healing is perfection . . . healing helps us grow . . . healing helps makes sense of what sometimes doesn't always makes sense . . . and most importantly, healing helps us to move forward.

I recently found myself in need of some major healing . . . for the past few months, I had been walking around in a bit of a fog. For me that meant being tired, on some levels feeling depressed, unsure of my next step, needing some sort of change in my life and not really caring . . . a general malaise. Although I had gone through feelings of being unsure various times in my life . . . I had never felt anything like this before. It totally sideswiped me. It was like I had these emotions come right up to the precipice, but without being able to identify and release them. It was very troubling. I very much wanted to come to terms with and release what was brewing inside of me. Once or twice the emotions started to surface only to be placed back in a holding position . . . all I knew was that I was unhappy and very much desired a clearing.

What were these emotions bubbling under the surface? Where they incidents from my childhood that needed identification, understanding and expulsion? Where they my true nature letting me know that I was a bit off of my path and that I needed to start taking care of myself better and reconnect with what brings me joy? Or was my driven nature and fears of not living up to my life's purpose starting to rebel because of my very tough nature on myself? It would be fair to say it was a combo of all three. Although in many ways, through the years I have done a nice job of finding balance, adventure and accomplishment . . . I realized more recently that I had lost my spark for living in the way that I used to have it. Although my creativity continued to come through for the most part in the form of books, movies and inspirational poetry . . . It had become a case of ok . . . what's next? I think what happened was that I so desperately wanted to help others through inspiring projects and writings . . . that I forgot to help and take care of myself; take care of my needs and relearn how to be the fun loving Brian that I used to know. I realized that I had reached a critical point . . . I wasn't happy, and as I like to tell others, If you aren't happy it's time for a change.

What was this change I was looking for? In my heart, I know that I am doing exactly what I am supposed to be doing . . . writing, creating inspirational projects and sharing what comes through me. Yet it wasn't making me happy — or at least I didn't think it was. But what I found out as I delved deeper was that the way I was going about it wasn't making me happy. I can tell you that nothing brings me more pure joy than when I am working on a film, self-help book, poem, or children's story. My projects just flow through me; like I am a conduit. But as I looked closer and paid attention . . . I noticed that my intuitive hits weren't coming in as frequently or as strong. It was as if I was driving with no headlights at night. I have always relied very much on my intuition for guidance. It was troubling not to be able to tap into it like I was used too. It was as if I didn't know what my next step would be . . . combine that with the emotional feelings that were bubbling under the surface needing release; I was in a tough spot.

At about this time I was headed up to Oregon where I am originally from for business. Well, the business was finished up a lot sooner than I had anticipated and as so often happens in life . . . our original plans get scrapped for something much more important and revealing. Although I originally travelled there for business . . . the real reason I went to Oregon was to heal.

My healing began when I went into a book store that I had been drawn to go visit. I was familiar with this store as I had done some workshops there on prior trips and had always enjoyed their staff; they were always very kind and open. I first asked if I could use one of their small "reading rooms" to meditate and think. They said no problem . . . I went back again the next day to do the same thing . . . the perceptive woman at the counter could tell that I was struggling a bit and that I needed to work something out. She suggested I have a session with a very talented intuitive healer that worked there. By rare chance she happened to have an opening that very same afternoon

. . . knowing that I was at wits end . . . I took the plunge and said sure. Let me just say that it was exactly what I had been looking for! Although I am a very self aware person . . . I knew I needed some assistance to dig deeper. During the session . . . she was definitely able to help me find, bring up and release a lot of what had been hanging around me . . . the caught energy, the misunderstood comments of yesteryear, the unworthiness that was living inside of me. I was able to begin the work of healing . . . this was what I was truly looking for.

I was able to identify some areas and issues that I had been carrying around with me for most of my life. She also helped me realize and identify my "true" need to add more play into my life; whether it was a bike ride, hike, hanging out with friends or a mini vacation. I had to incorporate that playfulness back into my life to allow everything to properly flow. And once I began to do that . . . I am happy to say that it was like I fell right back into being the real me. Life felt exciting again . . . I felt alive and because I felt alive I was able to tap back into my intuition and regain my creativity and intuition. I was also able to set aside a bit of my "go go go" nature, because I now knew that it wasn't working for me in the way that I was using it. I needed to get off the proverbial "hamster" wheel to replenish and regenerate through more play.

Take care of yourself friends . . . seek help to release the pains you have been holding onto . . . they need to be released and are way too big to carry around in your light; as it was with me . . . it held me back. I was stuck, I was depressed, I wasn't on my path. By being open to releasing what was stuck inside of me as well as learning how to play again I was able to free myself which in turn helped me to be myself. I want you to free yourself as well . . . be open to healing, be open to playing and be open to moving forward!

G. BRIAN BENSON 2012

Play

Light shines in and hearts open wide
As we follow bliss, let it guide

To reach new heights and comfort zones
Release the weight, pay off the loans

That hold us back, when we don't play
Instant freedom, each brand new day

Colors seem brighter, goodness grows
A smile drifts, from your head to toes

Worries are tabled, fears subside
Troublesome thoughts go off and hide

The mind's empty, freedom complete
Chance to renew, loving retreat

Creative flow, from higher realms
Speak truth through us and take the helm

In tune, aware, to every sound
No more searching, our soul is found

True prescription, in every way
To soar and be free, simply play

G. Brian Benson 2012

Love is not a specific act,
it is a way of being.

G. BRIAN BENSON

How Do Others Treat You?

One way that we can learn a lot about ourselves so that we can move forward, is to pay attention to how others treat us. Are you being treated with respect, courtesy and love; or with indifference, disrespect and disregard? I realize this is a bit of a harsh question, but I feel it is very important to think deeply and clearly about it. The information you can gather and learn from this question could truly set you free! I would like you to focus on the fact that the way others treat us is a mirror of how we feel about or treat ourselves. This is very much in line with my saying we all have the need to love and be loved. If we are neglecting ourselves (not loving ourselves unconditionally), how can we expect others to love and respect us?

If the way others treat us is a reflection or mirror of how we treat ourselves, then we really must take a closer look at how we treat ourselves. I want you to be hyper-aware of this. I would love it if you could dedicate some time to think about and process how you truly feel about yourself and how others treat you. Dig deep and trust your intuition (answers). If you find some things that make you uncomfortable, please don't be afraid. You are on the right track! Pat yourself on the back and be proud of the fact that you are showing yourself the love that you deserve!

You are worthy and you are worth it. Just imagine how much better you will feel allowing yourself to emulate your true loving nature. Not only will your life be more fulfilling, the love that you show yourself will be like a bright, shining beacon for all to see. And believe me when I say, that when your light is shining, it will allow others to shine back and show you the love and respect that you deserve! It will be the same love that you are proudly showing yourself.

G. BRIAN BENSON 2012

Need Some Motivation?

Having a bit of trouble finding ways to get motivated? Don't worry; it happens to all of us. Take a look at this handy list and implement its suggestions . . . you will be back on track in no time!

- Watch an inspirational show or movie — Need a quick pick-me-up? Turn on or pick up a copy of a favorite movie or show that inspires you. This is a guaranteed fix to get you feeling upbeat, inspired and motivated!

- Listen to music — Another great way to feel more motivated and change your attitude is by listening to music that inspires you.

- Get more sleep — Are you getting enough sleep? Getting more sleep will give you more energy; make you more productive and probably a much happier, motivated person!

- Go exercise — Need a little more energy through-out the day? Want to lose a few unwanted pounds? Want to think more clearly and be more produc-tive? Want to feel better about yourself and have more motivation? The answer is easy, get some exercise!

- Hang out with positive people — If you strive to be happy, inspired and motivated, like most of us do, you will also want to associate with people who aspire to the same goals.

- Try something new (take a chance) — If you are feeling unmotivated and going through the motions . . . the best way to snap out of your rut is to try something new! We aren't meant to be stagnant. We were put here to learn, have fun and grow. The world is your seriously your oyster!
- Eat better, eat less — Eat better, eat less . . . just like it sounds. What have you got to gain if you follow this mantra? More energy, motivation, a body that runs more efficiently, a longer life, higher self esteem and clothes that fit better, just to name a few. What's not to like about that!
- Laugh — Have you ever had one of those days where nothing seemed to be going right and then all of a sudden you saw or heard something really funny that just totally turned your attitude around because you started to laugh? We all have. Laughter really is the best medicine.
- Take a trip (get away) — Shake things up . . . get out of Dodge . . . even if it is just for the afternoon. It will replenish you.
- Clean house — How do you feel when you get home from work and notice your house or apartment is dirty or out of sorts? It feels heavy, right? Get rid of that burdensome feeling by tidying up and cleaning house. What might take only a short time will make a huge difference in your attitude and, more importantly, will free up your mind and let you truly relax and feel motivated for your next adventure.

There you go . . . 10 new ways to get the bounce back in your step and find the motivation to be the REAL you! Enjoy the process, keep an open mind and always expect the best. You deserve it!

G. BRIAN BENSON 2012

A Minute of Failure

A minute of failure can lead one to grow
Or tumble and stumble to the depths far below
The decision is yours, what to do when you fall
To pack up and quit or stand firm and tall

Everyone fails, it's natural and true
It's part of the process to grow and become new
So pick yourself up and give try again
If you find yourself failing, it's a fleeting trend

Don't give in to failure or you will never be set free
It's for those who don't believe, and lack vision to truly see
Keep standing; keep standing, each time you fall down
Your true nature will emerge, your spirit unbound

G. Brian Benson 2008

Don't be afraid to step out of your comfort zone.
Chances are you are going to land quite
comfortably with both feet on the
ground ready to take that next step.

G. BRIAN BENSON

Are You Paying Attention to What You Are Paying Attention To?

Have you ever really paid attention to what you pay attention to? Are you in control of what you are feeding your mind? In other words, what you tell yourself and what your course of action is and why? Or are you just going through the motions and letting old tapes and habits determine the course you are on? I like to call this "sleep walking through life."

It is so important to be consciously aware of what your thoughts are. It is so important to be aware of what you tell yourself and what you want your course of action to be. Why? Because the fact is, you control your own destiny. If you don't pay attention to what you are putting out there, then you leave yourself wide open to the whims and unbalanced nature of having indecisive thoughts or worse yet, letting others make choices for you.

Most of you have heard the phrases "thoughts are things" or "like attracts like." Well in the case of not paying attention to what you are thinking or saying to yourself you could be charting your course with indecisive, incorrect, unhealthy and possibly negative thoughts. Is that how you want your future to unfold? Probably not. If you are thinking negative or indecisive thoughts, then you will be potentially creating a negative or indecisive future.

However, if you start to pay attention to what you are telling yourself or thinking, you have the ability to change those thoughts and negative self-talk and replace it with positive thoughts and positive self-talk. You will then have the ability to create the life that you want and deserve. By paying attention to what you are paying attention to, you can steer your ship in any direction that you want to. Who wouldn't want that?

G. BRIAN BENSON 2009

You Are . . .

Capable and strong
As you move throughout your day
Kind and forgiving
In each and every way

Centered and balanced
Always grounded, calm and whole
Ready, called and sure
Stepping into your true role

Purpose and passion
They walk hand in hand for you
The love for yourself
Is your everlasting glue

Trusting your new path
Life's magic truly begins
Your bright light does shine
From gifts that come from within

Led by a knowing
Intuitions guiding plan
Your needs are now met
Relaxation is at hand

G. Brian Benson 2012

Creativity, love and nature are all fuel for the soul.

G. BRIAN BENSON

Is Your Foundation Solid?

I want you to take a second and really let that quote sink in . . . What does it mean to you? For me . . . it stresses the importance of loving yourself and how crucial that love is to really take off and live the life you deserve and were meant to live. If you don't love and accept yourself for the amazing and wonderful person you truly are, your foundation will be shaky as you go through life. What does a shaky foundation look like? It could mean many things. It could create a lack of confidence or belief in yourself in wanting to accomplish a goal or dream. It could bring out your insecurities in a relationship. Or it could leave you walking through life feeling unworthy and fearful because you feel that you aren't deserving of anything joyful. I don't want this to be the case for anyone!

This subject of people not really loving themselves like they should became very clear to me as I began to do an interactive workshop called "Unleash Your Dreams!" There is a section during the workshop where I ask everyone to take a minute and write down 5 things that they like about themselves. It could be anything . . . their eyes, their personality, their athletic accomplishments, etc. . . . I was very surprised when many of the workshop attendees said they couldn't come up with anything! My heart sank . . . I then tried to guide them to find a few items to put on their list. I mean I had no trouble seeing their gifts, but they did.

I immediately made a note to myself to focus on this section of my workshop in the future so I could try and help people who are standing on a shaky foundation because of a lack of love for themselves. I wanted them to see their gifts as well as realize how important it is . . . so they could unchain themselves and really move through life in love, joy, and living out their goals and dreams.

My work continues in trying to help others see their true inner-greatness. It resides within all of us, I can guarantee that. You just need to look inside and peel some layers to get there! And the very first thing and the most important thing that we can do is to truly love yourself. Once you can get there, the sky is the limit! I am going to do something that I have never done before in one of my blogs . . . I am going to leave you with a bit of homework today. Please take a few minutes and write down 5 things that you like about yourself. If you can come up with more . . . do it! And when you feel you are done, whether it is 1 item or 10 items . . . let them wash all over you and sink in to your being. They are truths and they will help you stand solid and firm on your own personal foundation. With that being the case . . . anything is possible!

G. BRIAN BENSON 2010

Reach Out

Believe in your dreams and make them come true
By staying on course and forging your view
Reach out and reach up, let the Universe know
Of what's in your heart, it's ready to flow!

Just believe and take action, start now today
Your intuition will guide you, every step of the way
Stay balanced, stay centered, and never give in
Your hard work will pay off, you're destined to win!

G. BRIAN BENSON 2007

Laughter is instant sunshine!

G. BRIAN BENSON

Remember When You Were a Kid?

Remember when you were a kid? If you were anything like me, you were lost in a land of make believe, playing a myriad of games and having loads of fun getting absorbed in the moment. Think back for a second and try to place yourself back on that prized bicycle or in that special tree house. Can you resonate with that feeling? How does it feel? There really is nothing like playing with your childhood friends without a worry in the world. Can you feel the lightness of the moment? Can you feel your worries just drift away? Can you feel the excited optimism and happiness that comes from hanging around your friends? It drifts in and out, back and forth while the warm sun stands watch over whatever game you happen to be playing that day.

This carefree lifestyle we led as kids; this carefree feeling that anything was possible. Where did it go? You know there is no reason that you can't tap back into that feeling. Just because you are older doesn't mean that it has to be lost forever. We can learn a lot from children and how they carry themselves. In all actuality, I think that to be able to regain that carefree, happy, optimistic, anything is possible feeling we had as kids is not only possible to regain, but it is a key component in maintaining our happiness, having a fulfilled life and creating and living out our goals and dreams.

How do we tap back into this feeling? How do we

regain that carefree nature that is open to possibility and being lost in the moment that kids have mastered? Here are some suggestions . . .

- *Go play.* It doesn't matter what . . . just go play! Grab a Frisbee and some friends and throw it around. Play a board game with your grand kids. Go shoot baskets at the local park basketball hoop. It doesn't matter what it is . . . just go play; get lost in the moment!
- *Let go of the urge to "do."* Let go of feeling like you always have to go do something. Sure we all have responsibilities as we get older . . . family, work, etc. But I am a firm believer that we create a lot of habits that aren't really that important. Identify them and let them go. Watching too much TV? Spending too much time on the Internet? Take some of that wasted time and go play! Not only will you gain the benefits of playing but you will also release some of the weight and pressure of your perceived "need" to do something.
- *Be in the moment.* Leave your to-do list at home. Just focus on what you are doing at that very moment. Let tomorrow's tasks stay in the future.
- *Hang around fun, positive people.* It's as simple as it sounds. Surround yourself with folks that already get it. If you are hanging out with fun, positive people it is only natural that some of their energy and fun nature rubs off on you!

- *Be open-minded.* Let go of any pre-conceived notions you have about yourself and what you are doing while you are playing. Many of us try so hard to maintain certain images of ourselves that keep us rigid, sometimes stuck and closed-minded. Be open to trying new things; be open to looking silly sometimes. It can be very freeing and look out . . . you just might like the way you feel!

So please . . . take a step back down memory lane and see, feel and remember what it was like to be a kid. Not only will it provide you with a new sense of purpose, but it will help you lead a much happier and healthier life as you shed some of the mental and emotional weight that you carry. Remember when you were a kid?

G. BRIAN BENSON 2012

Trust

Flowing and joyful, the way it should be
As we wander through life, trying to see

A life full of yearning, of goodness, of grace
Letting go of conflict, struggle, the race

It's easy to see with imperfect eyes
All that is synthetic, illusion, lies

It holds us back, caught up in that play
Against the grain, slow moving decay

Life, growth and love, always hand in hand
Accept each for their worth, all so grand

It doesn't have to sting, or even bite
Faith in the process, not in the fight

Your vision becomes clear, always to scale
Energies shifted, you blaze a new trail

Perfection exists, presence is key
Each moment treasure, sets you free

Trust in your path, step into the light
True nature soars and always takes flight

G. BRIAN BENSON 2012

Time to Go to the Paint Store?

In my first book *Brian's List*, there is a cartoon image of *me* spray painting myself with a can of "respect." I make mention of this because there is really nothing more important that we can do for ourselves than treat ourselves with respect. Treating ourselves with respect doesn't just mean positive self-talk and making sure others are treating us right. It means *we* need to treat ourselves right as individuals.

There are numerous ways we can treat ourselves with respect — being aware of what kind of food we put in our bodies, getting enough sleep, making sure we get some exercise and movement, as well as allowing for quiet time. Not only will you begin to thrive as you treat yourself better, everything else tends to fall into place as well; whether it is other positive people coming into your life, your intuition coming through stronger or things flowing at a much more even pace. Can you too paint yourself with a can of "respect?"

G. BRIAN BENSON 2012

Celebrate Your Wins!

As you begin to break out and live from your heart and follow your intuition, you are going to start noticing that things will begin to fall into place for you and that many little "wins" will occur on your way to living out your goals and dreams. I want to bring to your attention the importance of celebrating these "wins." When we begin to head down the path toward living out our dreams these "wins" and achievements are confirmations that we are going in the right direction! That we *are* making things happen and will continue to do so. By celebrating these events we are confirming to ourselves that we are on the right path and that we acknowledge and trust the information that we are receiving.

Plus, we can build on the confidence that we are receiving from our "wins," which will make it easier to take the next step in our desire to live out our dreams. "Wins" breed confidence which helps us move forward and breed more "wins."

Celebrating ourselves and our accomplishments is a lot of fun and helps us build self-esteem. You can never go wrong when you are honoring and loving yourself and the positive things you are doing. How does one celebrate? That is up to you. Some people like to have a party. Others might go to dinner at their favorite restaurant. You could buy yourself flowers or go to a movie. The list is endless.

I will admit that celebrating my "wins" wasn't the easiest thing for me to do. At times I can be very driven and I felt that I should continue moving forward at "light speed" to make things happen. Because of that, some of my "wins" weren't celebrated like they should have been. I worked hard on that though because I knew it was so important. One of my favorite ways to celebrate is to take a walk and imagine that there are hundreds of balloons and banners hanging from the trees that I walk past all saying "Way to go Brian!" or "Congratulations!" It is almost like having my own private parade! It doesn't matter how you celebrate your "wins," just do it! It lets the Universe know that you are open to more "wins" and celebrations on the way to living out your dreams!

G. Brian Benson 2009

You know the great thing about life I feel . . . is that
if you really consciously choose to . . . you can do
or create pretty much anything you want. Life is
basically one big blank chalkboard. But the problem
as I see it . . . is that not enough people are picking
up a piece of chalk and creating their story in their
own words. They are letting others do it for them.

G. BRIAN BENSON

There Once Was a Girl . . .

There once was a girl, whose eyes smiled to the world
As her spirit began to take flight
Her passions and goals became clear in her mind
Her life started feeling just right

Her heart shone bright, just like the sun
For all to see and inspire
Learning and sharing to help others along
They all became one, like a choir

Her fear now gone, her soul lifted up
Her senses felt alive and full of might
No more limits, only uncharted highs
Eyes now smiling, her future bright!

G. BRIAN BENSON 2003

Life is a wonderful administration of the heart, the mind and the soul. By listening to your heart and visualizing with your mind, you can come into alignment with your soul.

G. BRIAN BENSON

Awareness is the First Step

"Awareness is the first step toward personal freedom."
—Don Miguel Ruiz

Knowledge is power, pure and simple. As we learn, grow and become more self-aware our world opens up in amazing ways. We stop repeating harmful, never-ending cycles, we let go of others who aren't impacting our life in a positive, loving way and we get unstuck from our inaction of not knowing our true path. The beauty of being self-aware is that it is an ongoing process. We are here to learn and grow and when we are open to that task our lives become much more enjoyable and free. There are always people that come into our lives at just the right moment to help us learn, if we pay attention and listen. That is the key — paying attention to our daily interactions with people along with the self-talk that comes along with it. There is always a wealth of information coming through us at any given time.

When we find the areas where we keep "bumping into a wall" so to speak we can take a step back to figure out what it's about and why it keeps popping up. The intention is that by becoming aware of our limiting patterns, we can stop the same reoccurrences of pain from happening in the future. This pain may occur because we are letting our ego get in the way, or because we're playing the victim card or due to the negative, hurtful company we keep or even because of our own lack of self-esteem. The good news is — these are all areas we can improve on and even eliminate in our lives. Self-awareness helps us have healthier relationships (most likely because we aren't looking for our partner to make us happy — we know that it comes from within ourselves), it lets us understand where our fears come from (which in turn will help us release them) and it allows us to take flight to make a positive difference in our lives, as well as in all of the lives we touch.

As I work on my own self-awareness, I work to be in what I call the "observer" role. What this means is that I simply step outside of myself and watch my daily interactions from a distance — like someone standing next to me who is watching me in action. It helps me be rational and get to the core of the areas that I need to be more self-aware in. Since I have been working on myself for quite some time, I am able to draw on past experiences which I have filed away, and have allowed me to really get to know myself. This knowledge in turn helps me be a better me as I go through the second half of my life. Stuff happens to all of us, but it is our level of self-awareness that allows us to flow through it more easily and comfortably.

G. Brian Benson 2012

Keys to Life

To follow a dream is a noble task
That lines us up with our soul to bask
In the light that spreads to all mankind
Which sets us free, to break ties that bind

To forgive and let go is the greatest gift
You can give yourself to watch your spirit lift
Your life will move forward with the past behind
No obstructions, just production with a free flowing mind

What you say to yourself will seal your fate
Whether it's thoughts of love or words of hate
You map your course, no matter which route you choose
So pick quite wisely, you have everything to lose

Abundance will come to those who believe
It's all in how we act and perceive
Put stock in yourself and love what you do
Your life will be authentic, your vision true

To be non-judgmental is the trick
To view all others and make life truly click
It sends out a message there is love in your heart
Never again will you be separate or apart

To stay in balance, there's no better way
To flow through life and make use of each day
So take some time, to let yourself breathe
You will be amazed at what you'll receive

G. Brian Benson 2009

Your love for yourself is the bedrock that
your entire foundation stands upon.

G. BRIAN BENSON

Dream a Little Dream . . .

"Every great dream begins with a dreamer.
Always remember, you have within you the
strength, the patience, and the passion to
reach for the stars to change the world."
—Harriet Tubman

I want you to close your eyes for a few seconds . . . As you slowly open them; imagine yourself coming out of a foggy stupor . . . at first not knowing where you were or how you got there. And then imagine . . . realizing you are lying down on a cot covered in a blanket with an I.V. in your arm, and that you feel absolutely dead tired. And finally imagine a huge teeth-glaring smile come across your face, and a wave of relief combined with satisfaction as soon as you realize you know exactly where you are and wouldn't trade it for the world!

This is the feeling I had a few years back after finishing my 4th Ironman triathlon. And no they didn't all end that way! I think the 97 degree heat combined with my being somewhat under trained were the reasons I ended up in the medical tent that day. But the funny thing is (some people might call me crazy), I would do it again in a heartbeat. You know why? Because it was a dream of mine.

Do you have a dream you want to accomplish? Of course you do. So did I. We all have goals and dreams.

What is your dream and what is holding you back from attaining it? Is your dream at the forefront of your existence or has it been tucked away and forgotten? For starters let's get it back into your mindset and honor that your dream is something that is important to you and that you believe in. It isn't going to manifest itself. It needs fuel! Your dream is calling out to you and saying; make me a part of your life. Think about me! Believe in me! Bring me to fruition!

How can you feed your dream? What is the fuel that will make it go? First of all you must believe in your dream. You need to make it an important, integral part of your life. I mean you need to taste it! I want you to imagine what your life will feel like when your dream becomes a reality. Will you feel happy? Satisfied? Fulfilled? Of course you will! You know what else fulfilling your dream will do? It will give you the confidence to make another goal or dream become a reality. Why is this? Because you will have the momentum flowing from your initial realized goal or dream. I think you can see where this is going . . . each successful accomplishment will breed a stronger confidence within yourself which will lead to more success! Before you know it, you will be living a life of true fulfillment and actualized dreams. What more could you ask for?

G. Brian Benson 2010

The Star Painter

Way back in the beginning, before all that ever was
Lived a man with a kind hearted soul
His job was important, very serious indeed
It left his heart content, and quite full

His job was to create, and paint all the stars
Across the vast, wide ranging sky
He couldn't scrimp or hurry, each one quite unique
Like a snowflake, all one of a kind

His task wasn't simple; there was more to his job
That most folks didn't realize or know
You see each star had a purpose or role in one's life
Which helped truth and positivity flow

While painting each star with his special blend of paint
He would magically inspire a thought
The thought would then stick to the brand new star
Waiting for someone to be taught

Each star told a story, of happiness and hope
Of dreams that were going to come true
He took great care and gave much thought
To make each star bright, cheery and new

He wanted to assist, and give life meaning
To all those who wanted to learn
So he worked and he worked, painting both day and night
To him, quite important and of concern

He felt supported, to give was divine
It was the lesson he wished to teach all
So he gave as he painted, spreading peace, love and wonder
Staying true to his purpose, his call

He wanted to reward, those that believed
And followed their heart to their bliss
He knew it the key to have fulfillment in life
And certainly wanted no one to miss

Stay true to your heart and follow your dreams
And share what you have learned
Our friend the star painter would be proud
The world, much better in return

G. BRIAN BENSON 2004

Take Me Out to the Ball Game

So here we are at the end of another baseball season and a new World Series champion has been crowned. Although I absolutely love the playoffs, this time of the year has always been a bit sad for me. You see, I like baseball and let me tell you why. It's not the fresh air or highly skilled players, nor the smell of the grass and popcorn or its captivating history. It's not even the intellectual side of the game or the beautiful new architectural masterpieces that are called ballparks these days. I like baseball because it is a timeless game.

You see in baseball there are no clock, no 12 or 15 minute quarters and no halftime to speak of. It is timeless and full of possibility, just like our lives. Yes, there are 9 innings in a regulation game, but there are no rules that state how long those innings must go.

If you are anything like me caught up in society's drive to live your life by clocks and watches, marching from one task to another because of your schedule, you know and feel that it can weigh quite heavily on you. It is hard not to fall into this trap. Everything is based upon time in our lives. What time we need to wake up at, get to work by, what time school starts/ends, when we need to pick up our kids, etc. I think you get the picture. We are slaves to time. It is a subconscious pressure that is always nipping at our heels never really allowing us to be free.

Baseball isn't like that . . . baseball is on its own schedule. When you are at a baseball game you are taking a timeout from your busy life; you aren't looking at your watch or at a scoreboard that tells you how much time is left in the game. In other words you are living in the present moment.

Living in the present moment is the key to living a happy and fulfilled life. The beauty of baseball is that it sits comfortably in the gap between the past and the future . . . there is no feeling guilty about the past and fearing the future at a baseball game. Baseball allows us to focus on the here and now . . . baseball is timeless.

So yes, I also enjoy the sunshine, the smell of grass and popcorn as well as the high level of play . . . but they are all just icing on the cake for me. The real reason that I enjoy baseball is because I am able to forgot everything else in my life and just BE for the duration of the game. Too bad they don't play double headers anymore . . .

G. BRIAN BENSON 2010

Just remember the sun is always
shining behind the clouds.

G. Brian Benson

Moon Boy

There once was a boy who would look up in the sky
And focus his stare on the moon
He would ponder and think of the many ways
He could live his life in full bloom

His wishes and dreams known only to him
Were exciting and real in his head
Dreams of travel and adventure would swirl around
Until he fell softly asleep in his bed

The moon to him was a giant friend
To dream upon, this set him free
Free to think and grow and learn
Free for him to just be he

His moon was inspiring, a bright shining star
This sent his spirits to flight
When feeling low he'd look high in the sky
And then soon would be feeling alright!

His friendship with the moon helped plant a seed
Down deep inside his soul
This gave him the courage to be who he wished
And of his life take control

So believe in yourself and always keep on
With the help of your friends like the moon
The power is there, just open your mind
It will all come together quite soon!

G. BRIAN BENSON 2002

Be Yourself to Free Yourself!

Be yourself to free yourself . . . it really is as simple as it sounds. For us to be truly free in our lives, I mean truly free, we need to be our authentic selves. It means not comparing yourself to or wishing you were someone else. It means you aren't trying to be or act like someone else. It means you aren't living your life based on someone else's wishes or influence. Although in some parts of my life I was being truly authentic, I didn't step into who I was fully until after I left the family business and followed my heart into writing and filmmaking; creating positive, inspirational messages to share.

What "be yourself to free yourself" means is that you accept who you are and your capabilities. It also means you are open to learning about yourself as well as tapping into and sharing your gifts. "Be yourself to free yourself" is holding your intentions in your heart, while having an open mind and no expectations of how you are going to reach those intentions. It also means that you find balance in your life and treat yourself with respect. It's honoring your goals and dreams and not being afraid to step outside of your comfort zone to reach them. It also means that your light is shining very bright as you move through your authentic, fulfilled life because you are aligning with your true self.

Where are some areas of your life that you aren't being truthfully authentic with yourself?

Please, please, please . . . be yourself to free yourself!

G. BRIAN BENSON 2011

Your Voice

Your voice creates a ripple
O'er the land and well beyond
Truthful words vibrate lifted
To create a loving bond

Your voice can be your freedom
Or your voice can be your hell
Mindful heed in word and thought
Send forth love and light to gel

Your voice can give permission
To another seeking truth
Authentic, centered, living
Tap's into eternal youth

Your voice can be the difference
To set a young child free
Loving words to encourage
A model for them to be

Your voice is your true freedom
When it's spoken from the heart
Intuition's guiding path
Helps you play your destined part

Your voice gives inspiration
For those too afraid to speak

Reassuring tones shared true
Will help others gain their peak

Your voice is your ready key
To unlock your truthful worth
Spoken pure, life now renewed
Energized, loving, re-birth

Your voice is fundamental
For all life and love to flow
Empowered, valued, perfect
Painting a worldly glow

G. Brian Benson 2012

To truly open your heart is to
remember who you truly are.

G. BRIAN BENSON

Something to Think About . . .

Last week I was feeling a bit under the weather . . . absolutely no energy and a bit of a sore throat. I believe it was because I ran myself down. Some of you might know the routine . . . you go and try to do much and not allow yourself to regenerate. We all fall prey to being sick now and then, whether it was because we picked it up from someone else or in my case push yourself into being forced to slow down. The end result is the same. You feel tired, crappy and wish that you could have your normal energy level back. That is the world that I was living in for most of the week. I would like to think it was the Universe's way of telling me to slow down because I wasn't listening to the warning signals via my intuition. Whatever the case, it got me thinking. You see I had plenty of time to do that in between long bouts of sleep and the double dose of movies that I watched daily because I didn't have the energy to do anything else. What was I thinking about you ask? Well, being a bit of an analytical person, there was a couple of things that I wanted to understand better.

The first thing that I wrapped my brain around was the fact that I noticed some of my fears were tremendously being magnified while I was sick. I am normally a very positive, optimistic person through and through as all of you who know me would attest; but during a span of 2 or 3 days I was struggling big time.

Why was I struggling? I was struggling because I began to worry about things that were out of my control and things that weren't normally relevant. Why was this? Was it because I was feeling weak, tired and vulnerable? Was it because I wasn't in my normal daily routine which included exercise, being outdoors and meditation? Was it because I felt like I was missing out on the wonderful possibilities that normally lay before me each day while I lay in bed and watched movies not having any energy to leave my house? Or was it because I now wasn't in control of my life because of the weak nature I was in. I came to the conclusion that it was a combination of all them with a heavy tilt toward not being in control of my life. Here I was, feeling weak and helpless because I couldn't control my situation. Normally I am out in the world daily controlling every aspect of what I do relying on my inner guidance and intuition to guide me. But here I lay, feeling fatigued, weak and definitely not in control. It is a feeling that I don't like and never want to get used to. But then it hit me . . . as I looked back to the week prior to my having fallen sick, I wasn't allowing my guidance and intuition to lead me. I remembered that I was trying to force things and control things that weren't really resonating deep down inside me. There is a very distinct difference. When we allow our intuition and guidance to come through and lead us, we flow along smoothly and effortlessly. When we try to control things, force things, and push things into place, we become out of balance, fearful and potentially run down just like I experienced. Although I felt like I already knew this, it was a huge wake up call to continue to trust my intuition and inner guidance although I had temporarily allowed myself to forget this very important lesson.

Which leads me to the other thing that I am trying to wrap my brain around . . . ever notice that when you get sick you do all kinds of things (lots of sleep, eat better, vitamins, rest, drink lots of fluids) to get well again and then when you are well you do all kinds of things (not enough sleep, eat not so healthy, go and neglect rejuvenation time) that can make you sick? Something to think about . . .

G. BRIAN BENSON 2010

Live for inspiration . . . there is nothing better than
tapping into something that lifts you up,
gives you hope and makes you want to
be the best for yourself and others!

G. BRIAN BENSON

Believe

When you wish upon a star
Your heart and mind, in sync go far
Dream your dreams and follow bliss
Souls on target to never miss

Sail your ship; let your wings take flight
Your heart's open to spirit's light
Love abounds for all who believe
Ask; hold trust and you shall receive

G. BRIAN BENSON 2007

Truth Be Told,
What Is Your Pain Threshold?

A very good friend of mine once said that "death creates awareness." I find myself really understanding what she meant as I mourn the loss of a very dear friend whose life tragically ended not quite 2 weeks ago. Michael Kendall was a friend to many, a teacher, a messenger of truth and most importantly a student.

We are all students in the scheme of life, but what made Michael stand out was that he tried to help others learn from his past mistakes. Michael was the co-author of a fantastic book called "A Truthful Opportunity." In his book he bared his soul and became absolutely transparent in relating his life's mistakes and how they transformed him into the person that he was before he passed. His message was truth. His message was speak your truth and you will be set free. No more hiding behind one's fears and perceived inabilities through lies. They just create more of the same until you absolutely forget who you are and what you are here to do.

I would like to include an excerpt from Michael's book "A Truthful Opportunity" as a tribute to a wonderful person who left many friends behind as well as to share his wisdom that came from many dark days early on in his life that made him into the transparent, loving person that we all cared very deeply for.

Pain directs us to the truth when we are disconnected. Pain is only necessary for those who choose not to see or hear what God has given them. This is why not everyone encounters the same amount of pain in life. Some only need to be gently nudged in order to walk through the door where awareness and light exist on the other side. Others will not move, so the pain becomes greater in order to push them through the door. Pain appears when we have placed ourselves so far in the darkness that we can't see and we use it to light the way. The longer you stand in the darkness, the greater the pain. My pain pushed me into the light. I connected to the truth of the seen and unseen world around me, finding my place in it.

Pain is a tool. It's one of the many that we have available to us. Throughout my life, my pain had nudged me forward many times, but more often than not I had chosen to deny it. Before, I had always chosen to keep my fear of looking at my pain in the back of my closet; knowing that I could retreat into my closet, away from this light, offered an inept solace. Now, the truth and all it represented radiated a loving light that encompassed me in an incredible powerful way. I wasn't accustomed to feeling connected to my pain. Its power was unmistakable. Sometimes, when I stepped out of the darkness into the bright light, my eyes hurt from the glare. I wanted to retreat.

But when I looked more closely, I realized it was the light that I needed and the darkness I feared. Now I knew I had to go further. If I didn't do this, I would continue to find ways to disconnect in order to deny my pain, instead of progressing along the new path I had begun. Live long enough in a frame of mind and it becomes a reality.

Peace to you Michael.

G. Brian Benson 2009

Set your intention and let the Universe
decide how you are going to reach it.

G. BRIAN BENSON

Arizona Dreams

Dreams . . . we all have them. They fuel our existence, they let us ponder on a brighter future, and the path to realize them fills our lives with excitement, fulfillment and growth. I want to share a story with you from an experience I had where I wasn't sure if I was going to be able to realize a dream of mine . . . It was back in 2006 and I was entered to race in Ironman Arizona which was being held in Tempe near Phoenix.

I found myself at the race start treading water with 2,300 other people in Tempe Town Lake. 2,300 hundred other people! Now, I don't know if any of you have participated in or witnessed a triathlon mass swim start with 2,300 people . . . but I can tell you one thing . . . it isn't pretty! To try and help you visualize what I am talking about . . . imagine a massive piranha feeding frenzy! It is one large mass of arms and legs flailing about . . . folks getting kicked in the head, goggles getting knocked off . . . the first 10 minutes are a bit scary to say the least!

Alright, so here I am at the start of the race right after the cannon went off . . . I had always been a good swimmer and had not expected any problems . . . well as it turns out . . . I started having a panic attack. I began to hyperventilate and have a lot of anxiety and felt an urgent need to try to swim over to the side of the lake. So after a terrifying handful of minutes of trying to keep my head above water and working my way sideways through a tangled mass of swimmers I got over to the side. First thing I did was take some deep breaths . . . and then I tried to make sense of what just happened. I was confused, scared and anxious all at the same time. Confused as to why it had happened and scared that I might not be able to continue and finish the race and accomplish my yearlong goal . . . luckily for me the deep breathing exercises really helped my anxiety begin to pass. After a few more minutes of relaxing, I then made my way back out into the water and proceeded to complete the swim portion.

For a moment though . . . I didn't know if I would be able to . . . My whole Ironman dream that I trained for, visualized and made sacrifices in my life for a whole year almost didn't happen. I can tell you that the feeling of triumph, relief, happiness, joy and fulfillment felt even sweeter when I crossed the finish line 13 hours later after the terrifying start to my day . . . I felt like I knew how I was going to reach the finish line that day, but life as it sometimes does . . . threw a wrench in my works with the panic attack. I had to re-focus and allow things to unfold a bit differently than I had originally planned. I still accomplished my goal because I held that intention . . . but I just had to be open to take a different road to get there.

You are no different . . .

G. BRIAN BENSON 2010

Who you are today, is not who you were yesterday and who you will be tomorrow.

G. BRIAN BENSON

Believing Eyes

Limber thoughts of trust present
New ways to live which heaven sent

Our hearts and minds a mix to stir
This yields results both inner and pure

Each path is new yet spoken for
To unlock our duty we must open the door

To listen and hear through believing eyes
And not be afraid when old ways die

To tap your highest, there's no greater score
Inspiration, motivation and love ever more

G. BRIAN BENSON 2007

Self-Appreciation 101

With the holidays upon us and in full swing, it is not uncommon to see newspaper articles or television programs reminding us about the importance of thinking about others or lending a hand to those in need. Now I am in total agreement with that premise. I have always said that the full measure of our personal happiness is dictated by how much we offer of ourselves in helping others. My wish however would be that these same newspapers and television programs reminded us about that all year, not just during the holiday season. So with that being said . . . please go do what you can to help others in any way that you are able to, it is the right thing to do and does make a difference. But I also want you to be aware of helping someone else out during this holiday season . . . *yourself!*

I don't know about you, but I sometimes forget to remember and appreciate all of the wonderful things that make up who I am and what I am about . . . not to mention all of the blessings and joys that are in my life and continue to show themselves. I know that I am not alone in this. Each and every one of you has amazing traits, characteristics and gifts that you have been given or developed! Not to mention many blessings that are in or a part of your life. You know this don't you?

For those of you who may have temporarily forgotten your greatness and the greatness that surrounds you, I invite you to do six fun and easy assignments. Do them all at once or spread them out; your choice. But be prepared to un-wrap the greatest Christmas gift that you will have ever received . . . *yourself!*

OK, it's simple . . . I want you to take a piece of paper for each category and I want you to list as many things as you can under each heading. That's it! There is no wrong or right answer; get creative. If you are having trouble email me and I will help. All I ask is that you really stretch your mind and put down whatever comes to you. You will be amazed at how much you have to be thankful for and how truly *amazing* you are.

- *Everyday miracles I take for granted*
- *The uncanny powers I possess*
- *The small joys that occur so routinely I forget how much they mean to me*
- *The steady flow of benefits bestowed on me by people I know and don't know*
- *What works for me*
- *What makes me feel at home in the world*

Remember your love for yourself is the bedrock that your entire foundation stands upon. When your foundation is strong, you can be anything and do anything that you put your mind to! Including appreciating yourself . . .

G. BRIAN BENSON 2010

You can only be your best for others,
when you are rested and whole yourself.

G. BRIAN BENSON

Connecting Is Everything

In today's fast paced, instant gratification, super-size me world, where people's lives are broken down and validated into bite size tweets, it's real easy to forget to take a long deep breath and remember what life is really all about . . . it's about people. It's about people and how much we all really have in common. We all have hopes and dreams . . . we all have fears . . . we all go through struggles and make mistakes, we all want to be heard and acknowledged . . . but most importantly, we all want to love and be loved.

It seems like our days are spent being surrounded by other people whether it be at school, work, the gym or the grocery store. But how well do we really get to know these other folks? Are we making an effort to do so? Or are we too busy to even notice?

You know . . . we all have stories. We all have unique experiences that make each and every one of us different from everyone else . . . and sometimes when we listen to other people's stories, it has a way of making our stories richer and more valuable.

How does listening to other people's stories have a way of making our lives and our stories richer? If we really paid attention we would find many similarities in their lives which might mirror ourselves and give us insight into how we can live our lives in a more fulfilling, inspired and enjoyable way. We might also find that they have gone through many of the same trials and tribulations that we have. We might even find that they have many of the same interests. There are many reasons why we may have something in common with someone else. We just have to do a little digging to find out. I can assure you it will be worth it.

So the next time you give your money to a cashier at the store, drive by some folks asking for help on the side of the road, or make a deposit to the clerk at your bank . . . just remember that they are people too and more than likely share many bonds, fears and interests with you, and by getting to know them your life may become richer and more satisfying. Connecting is everything.

G. Brian Benson 2011

There's Only One You

Believe in yourself, there's only one you
You were perfect and whole from the start
Proper thoughts every day, won't lead you astray
But send guidance and love from your heart

Believe in your dream, and it's bound to come true
Send it peace, send it hope, send it love
Through the power of your steadfast desire
You can manifest this gift from above

Believe in your path and trust in the gift
That your heart will lead the way
Others will see your belief in yourself
And will follow your lead every day

G. BRIAN BENSON 2007

If it feels right in your heart,
it is right.

G. BRIAN BENSON

Relax Into It

I had the pleasure last week to listen to author Noel Levine speak and although I took many lessons and received much enjoyment from his conversational style . . . the message that stuck with me the most came about while he was explaining how to just let go and RELAX into meditation to eliminate the mind chatter that we can receive while trying to meditate. Now this in and of itself is a great reminder for those of us who find meditation helpful, but occasionally challenging because we have trouble turning off this chatter; I appreciated the reminder to just "relax into" my meditation instead of force it. But I took something else from his suggestion . . . I immediately used his "relax into it" suggestion to another issue that I had been having. For the last couple of months, I have been having quite a bit of pain due to a minor medical condition and I felt that his words "relax into it" were meant exactly for me and what I have been going through. I begin to envision the area that I was having some pain in, took a few breaths and as I slowly let them out I allowed them to sink or "relax" into that pain. I immediately began to feel some relief. I then also realized that I had been focusing on and holding onto that pain up until that moment. You know keeping thoughts of "when is it going to stop?" "Will it ever stop?" "When will the relief come?" And because of the nature of those questions . . . I repeatedly reinforced that it was an issue in my life because I was focusing on it.

I then remembered a quote that I heard Wayne Dyer share once that said "what we embrace strengthens us and what we fight weakens us." I had been fighting my pain, I had been complaining about it, focusing on it and giving it more power than it deserved. I now realized that I needed to embrace or "relax into it"; knowing that it wouldn't be a part of my life forever and it too would come to pass.

You know pain is just one area where we can "relax into" something to make it better. What are some areas in your life that you would benefit from "relaxing into?" Your job, relationships, parenting, and loving yourself are just the tip of the iceberg. Fighting instead of embracing and "relaxing into" these examples just gives these areas more power and with more power they just make our lives frustrating and more difficult. If we relax into our issues, we are able to minimize or diffuse their hold on us. We are then able to more fluidly move through them and on with our lives which in turn will help us eventually work through what has us troubled. Where are you having some resistance in your life? Relax into it and see what happens . . .

G. Brian Benson 2011

Don't underestimate the power of getting outside!

G. Brian Benson

When I'm Just Me

I have no clue as to what to do
With my remaining days here on earth
Although I've been many places, and done many things
It can be easy to overlook my worth

So I struggle and tug, instead of nurture and hug
What's got me spinning inside
Then I lose all sight and give up the fight
And let others for me decide

But if I try to get clear, and put away my fear
I then see what I really could be
Not a doctor or mechanic, or someone in panic
But what I could be is just me

For when I'm just me, I can do as I please
I don't have to put up with any strife
I can think and take action, without any traction
And be happy with the way I live life

G. Brian Benson 1994

A Gift from an Unlikely Place

I had the honor of doing one of my workshops ("An Introduction to Balance") recently to a group of 21 teenage boys who were incarcerated at a youth correctional facility. The beauty of my workshops is that they are a bit different each time because of their interactive nature and the flow of the different participants that come through. What I witnessed that day while presenting to these young men will stick with me for a very long time. I had no idea what to expect or what kind of reaction I would get from them and basically was a bit nervous that there wouldn't be very much interaction. What happened totally blew me away.

Instead of having a lot of silence and looks of "why am I here" from the youth, I found many very intelligent young men who couldn't wait to speak and share their experiences, their regrets and their dreams. The depth of some of the youth was quite amazing to behold. Some talked of already having forgiven their peers who played a part in having them incarcerated in the first place. Many talked about how they wanted to go to college and how they were going to make it happen. Some talked about wanting to raise healthy families even though it wasn't something that was modeled for them while they grew up. Others talked about forgiving themselves for the crimes that they committed so that they could move forward. And finally a few youth made mention that they had separated themselves from their mothers or fathers, brothers or sisters, and friends to get away from their past of violence, crime, abuse and gang interaction.

I even had one teen tell me how he wanted to eventually be a youth counselor so he could help others like himself break free of their pasts and lead healthy futures. He told me that although he had no credits toward his high school degree when he was incarcerated, in two years he had almost completed his high school degree and would be able to start taking some college level classes. He then went on to tell me some of the pressures he is facing to make that dream happen. Apparently a friend of his and member of the gang he used to be a part of was recently shot by a rival gang member. The rival gang member was caught by the police and may possibly be sent to the same facility where the teen is incarcerated. The teen has received letters from the leader of his gang telling him he needs to take care of or avenge his friends shooting when the rival gang member arrives. He shared with me that he is really feeling a lot of pressure internally to honor his gang's wishes. But for him to keep his "eye on the prize" of helping others and getting his college degree he needs to look the other way. I can only imagine how difficult it is for him. His mom is even hoping that he doesn't go "soft" and takes care of his gang business. All I can say is wow . . . Children normally look to their parents for guidance, love and good advice. Can you imagine having your parents tell you something that in your heart you know is wrong and that it could affect your life forever? I certainly can't. Here's to hoping that he does that right thing.

I left that facility after the workshop feeling blessed in many different ways. Blessed that I had a healthy and happy childhood. Blessed that I didn't have as many obstacles to face to reach my goals and dreams as many of these young men do. Blessed that I had the opportunity to hopefully play a small role in helping these teens learn a bit more about themselves and give them some hope for their future. And blessed that I had the humbling opportunity to learn from them and realize what a gift freedom and choice is; something that they currently don't have.

Here's to hoping that all of these teens are able to turn their lives around and lead happy, productive lives when they get out. Unfortunately the odds don't support my hopes. However after listening to many of them yesterday and feeling their energy and spirit rise in their voices; I am confident that some will. If a troubled youth from a violent and abusive past can make their dreams and goals come true . . . why can't those of us who haven't had the setbacks that they have make our goals and dreams come true? Something to think about.

G. BRIAN BENSON 2010

I have found that I am happiest when I am being
creative . . . letting Source, God, The Universe . . .
whatever you want to call it, come through.
It is one of the few times when I know I am doing
exactly what it is I am supposed to be doing and
I can get out of my head and just be at total peace.

G. BRIAN BENSON

How Will I Make it Happen?

You know what? It's alright that you aren't sure how you will make your dream happen. All that matters initially is that you have a dream and are committed to making it happen. Once that is established, start moving forward! What does moving forward mean? Anything and everything! It just depends on what you need to manifest your dream. Do you need some money to finance it? Go figure out how to raise the money, whether it's from a part-time job or convincing others to back you. Do you need to educate yourself about a certain topic? Go take a class or talk with an expert on the subject. It's alright to ask questions and learn from those who do know! Do you need to get hands-on to begin to start writing or creating? What are you waiting for? Make it happen!

Let me give you a personal example. After having made it through my first 2 years of racing in triathlons (1987–88), I knew that I enjoyed it immensely and that it gave me a lot of confidence and pride. I still wanted to improve. I have always wanted to do the best that I can in pretty much anything that I have attempted.

I got this notion that my swimming needed to improve. I was a better than average swimmer but wanted to work on it nonetheless. I was working as a lifeguard at Oregon State University during some of their swim classes and noticed the women's swim team come in one time following a class I watched over. That got me thinking. I knew that the women's team was a funded university sport and I had heard that they had a men's swim club that wasn't. It was participant funded. I then began to wonder who was on the men's team and could anyone join? After some inquiries, I realized that anyone could join. I knew right then and there that was my answer to become a better swimmer; I joined. I didn't really know at the time what I was getting myself into. My triathlon swim training basically consisted of me jumping in the pool and swimming lap after lap. Maybe I would throw in some kickboard work. That was about it.

Well that was all about to change very quickly at swim practice. Everybody who was on the team had been a very proficient swimmer in high school and was quite fast and talented. Here I was . . . someone whose swim career consisted of a handful of triathlons and some summer swim lessons as a youth. I was terrified! Luckily for me the coach of the team was a supportive and wise man who had been coaching for a very long time. He understood where I was coming from and welcomed me.

No more jumping in the pool and swimming lap after lap for me. It was time for lung burning intervals and utilizing swim strokes that I had never attempted before! That first day while huffing and puffing my way through practice, I really began to wonder what I got myself into. Although quitting was an option that I honestly did think about, I decided to go again the next day. The routine was the same . . . lung busting interval after lung busting interval, but I began to realize that I could handle it. Sure I was the slowest swimmer there, but I knew that I could handle it! I also began to realize that there was no way I couldn't get faster if I stuck with this. So that is what I did. Although practices were always tough, I began to get faster and more confident day after day. It was a wonderful feeling indeed. I even went on road trips with them to swim meets and competed in the freestyle events (that is the stroke that is used for triathlon). Although I got my butt kicked in the meets by all the experienced and accomplished swimmers, it was exhilarating.

The key is to just start the process. And you know what? It's alright if you aren't quite sure what step #2 is. Just get started on step #1. The Universe has a wonderful way of providing us with what we need at the exact moment that we need it. Help is always on the way! Just know that it will come, and be open to it. You don't want to make the mistake of not being open to outside help or thinking that you can do it all by yourself. Anyone who has ever been successful in any field has had help from others along the way. Always remember that. Please don't let the fact that you aren't sure how you are going to make your dream happen hold you back. *Stay focused, believe and keep moving forward!*

G. BRIAN BENSON 2012

Sometimes our original plans get scrapped for something much more important and revealing.

G. Brian Benson

Awake

Awake my energy, guiding spark
Send me soaring; to purpose, on mark
Alert, alive to all that can be
Seeking, shining; as far as I see

Awake my mind, you bittersweet tool
Which leads one true or to play the fool
Weakened thoughts grasp, away from the core
Leave us tired, hungry, wanting more

Awake myself to who I can be
Uncluttered vision resides in me
Potential and greatness that is I
There are no limits under the sky

Awake myself to my truthful worth
Love, light, perfection; peace, joy and mirth
Creative fire; gifts deep inside all
Intuition beckons, heed its call

Awake my heart and step into love
Melt away young scars and rise above
Confusions kiss, once led me astray
I turn to myself to mute the grey

Awake my truth, thy grand unmasked self
Hidden, buried, found; authentic wealth

Our life's purpose, comfort, joy and ease
Guidance from within, eager to please

Awake my spirit, fears set aside
Soul's perfection, fervent, loving guide
Flowing love, our birthright, path, desire
Flame burns bright from this heavenly fire

G. BRIAN BENSON 2012

10 Mantras to Live By

Here are 10 powerful mantras I wrote that I want to share with you. They help bring balance, happiness and a sense of peace to my life every day. These 10 mantras are already hardwired into each and every one of us. It is just a matter of making the effort to reconnect and implement them. I hope that they bring peace, harmony and a sense of true wellbeing to you as well. — Sincerely, Brian

1)   I will listen to my heart. I will follow what it says and stay true to its message.

Our heart or intuition never gives us false messages. It is divine guidance leading us if we are willing to listen.

2)   I will be true to myself and follow my own life's meaning.

Not what someone else thinks or wants it to be for me! Only I can know what is right for me. I know this by following my joy and listening to my inner guidance.

3)   I will love and be non-judgmental to all others.

There are many different paths and many different lessons to be learned. What might work for me might not be true for another. We are here to guide and assist each other to be the best that we can be; but with the understanding that each one of us holds the key to reaching our own goals and tapping into our highest being.

4) I will not be afraid to do what is required.

Life is about growing, learning and remembering who we truly are. Without growth, we risk living an unfulfilled and stagnant life.

5) I will lay my ego down and remember that true nobility lies not in being better than anyone else, but in being better than I used to be.

We are all connected. There is no one better than I and no one less than I.

6) I will use forgiveness to free myself from what otherwise would hold me back or down.

Without forgiveness we become stuck. It is imperative that we release the anger, hurt, misunderstanding or confusion. It is poison in our system. That doesn't mean that we need to forget. But we must forgive.

7) I will believe in myself and believe in all of the loving forces that support me in my journey.

We are all perfection. And because of this fact, we all have total control of our lives, through our thoughts and actions. We all have guidance and support to get us where we are supposed to be. Believe!

8) I will love and accept myself for exactly who I am.

All the polished parts of myself as well as the unpolished parts; total acceptance. Until we love and accept ourselves, we make it much harder to be loved and accepted by others.

9) I will mirror the image of God (the Loving Universal Life Force) to all whom I come into contact with and meet.

May all of the peace and love that resides within me be seen by all whom I come into contact with. So that they may look into themselves and share all of the peace and love that lies within them.

10) I will respect and nurture all that resides within our natural world.

All of life is beautiful and wonderful in its own way. The earth and all of its interesting creatures that live upon it are linked together and help contribute to its perfection. Let us appreciate all.

G. BRIAN BENSON 2008

To learn more about Brian and his other books and projects as well as sign up for his free monthly newsletter go to

www.gbrianbenson.com

Brian's first book, *Brian List — 26 ½ Easy to Use Ideas on How to Live a Fun, Balanced, Healthy Life!* was the winner of the 2009 Next Generation Indie Book Award in the Self-Help category. It was also an Award-Winning Finalist in the Self-Help Motivational Category of the National Best Books 2009 Awards, sponsored by USA Book News.

Made in the USA
Charleston, SC
22 January 2013